DINOSAUR WARS

ALLOSAURUS

★★★★★★★★★★

VS

BRACHIOSAURUS

★★★★★★★★★★

MIGHT AGAINST HEIGHT

Michael O'Hearn

Consultant:
Mathew J. Wedel, PhD
Paleontologist

Raintree

www.raintreepublishers.co.uk
Visit our website to find out
more information about
Raintree books.

To order:
☎ Phone 0845 6044371
🖷 Fax +44 (0) 1865 312263
🖳 Email myorders@raintreepublishers.co.uk

Customers from outside the UK please telephone +44 1865 312262

Raintree is an imprint of Capstone Global Library Limited, a company incorporated
in England and Wales having its registered office at 7 Pilgrim Street, London,
EC4V 6LB – Registered company number: 6695582

Text © Capstone Press 2010
First published in hardback in the United Kingdom by Capstone Global Library in 2011
Paperback edition first published in the United Kingdom by Capstone Global Library in 2012
The moral rights of the proprietor have been asserted.

Editors: Aaron Sautter and Laura Knowles
Designer: Kyle Grenz
Media Researcher: Marcie Spence
Art Director: Nathan Gassman
Production Specialist: Laura Manthe
Illustrations by Philip Renne and Jon Hughes
Originated by Capstone Global Library Ltd
Printed and bound in China by South China Printing Company Ltd

ISBN 978 1 406 21818 3 (hardback)
14 13 12 11 10
10 9 8 7 6 5 4 3 2 1

ISBN 978 1 406 22086 5 (paperback)
15 14 13 12 11
10 9 8 7 6 5 4 3 2 1

British Library Cataloguing in Publication Data
A full catalogue record for this book is available from the British Library.

Acknowledgements
We would like to thank the following for permission to reproduce photographs: Shutterstock
parchment backgrounds (Valery Potapova), **stylized backgrounds** (Leigh Prather).

CONTENTS

WELCOME TO DINOSAUR WARS!

Dinosaurs were brutal creatures. They fought each other and ate each other. Usually it was meat-eater versus plant-eater or big versus small. But in Dinosaur Wars, it's a free for all. Plant-eaters attack plant-eaters. Giants fight giants. And small dinosaurs gang up on huge opponents. In Dinosaur Wars, any dinosaur battle is possible!

In this dinosaur war, Allosaurus and Brachiosaurus bash it out. You'll see how Allosaurus hunts dinosaurs much larger than himself. You'll discover how both dinosaurs fought and defended themselves. You'll learn about their very different weapons. Then you'll see them battling head-to-head – and you'll get to watch from a front row seat!

Allosaurus (AL-oh-sore-us)
Brachiosaurus (BRĂK-ee-oh-sore-us)

THE COMBATANTS

ALLOSAURUS
VS
BRACHIOSAURUS

Allosaurus might have hunted Brachiosaurus. Both dinosaurs lived in the same parts of the world. They lived in western North America, Portugal, and parts of Africa. Allosaurus **fossils** have also been found in Australia. Both beasts lived at the same time, too. Allosaurus lived from about 153 to 135 million years ago. Brachiosaurus lived from about 155 to 140 million years ago.

Brachiosaurus was one of the largest dinosaurs ever. In fact, he was so large that he had to spend most of his time eating. With all that meat on his bones, he would have looked like a delicious meal to a hungry Allosaurus.

While he was alive, Allosaurus was the largest **predator** on earth. But even the fiercest Allosaurus would have a hard time killing the giant Brachiosaurus. He would need some help. Some scientists think Allosaurus may have hunted in packs. Being part of a pack could have helped Allosaurus take down a Brachiosaurus.

While he was alive, Allosaurus was one of the most common dinosaurs on Earth. Scientists have found more fossils of Allosaurus than any other large predator.

FIERCE FACT
COMMON PREDATORS

fossil remains of an animal preserved as rock
predator animal that hunts other animals for food

SIZE

Allosaurus was a big, powerful predator. He weighed up to 3.2 tonnes. He measured about 12 metres (40 feet) long from head to tail and stood about 5 metres (16 feet) tall. That's about as heavy as a small elephant and as long as a bus. This might sound big, but Allosaurus was much smaller than the enormous Brachiosaurus.

Brachiosaurus means "arm lizard". He was given this name because of his unusually long front legs.

Brachiosaurus measured up to 30 metres (98 feet) from head to tail. He stood up to 15 metres (50 feet) tall, which is about as tall as a weeping willow tree. His long neck made up about half of his total body length. Because his front legs were longer than his back legs, his neck and body slanted upwards. Brachiosaurus was extremely heavy at 45 tonnes. He weighed about as much as 10 elephants. Brachiosaurus would have a definite size advantage against Allosaurus.

DEFENCES

Allosaurus
Powerful jaws

★ ★ ★

★ ★ ★

Brachiosaurus
Gigantic size

Wherever he went, Allosaurus was the scariest, most aggressive dinosaur around. Allosaurus didn't have armour or a club on his tail. His snarling mouth full of sharp teeth was the only defence he needed.

Over many years, the "long neck" dinosaurs like Brachiosaurus evolved to huge sizes to protect themselves from predators. However, the meat-eaters adapted by growing larger too.

FIERCE FACT

HUGE SIZES

Brachiosaurus was too big to pick on. His massive size was his main defence. Brachiosaurus probably travelled in **herds** for defence. If one giant dinosaur was too much to take down, then a whole herd of them would really be a challenge.

herd group of the same kind of animal

ALLOSAURUS' WEAPONS

Allosaurus' mouth was perfectly designed for chomping on meat. His jaw was flexible, and his skull was especially strong. Allosaurus had a gaping bite that could fit around the thickest body parts of his **prey**.

FIERCE FACT

FOSSILS

Only about three per cent of dinosaur fossils belong to meat-eaters.

Allosaurus' mouth held more than 50 teeth, some as long as knives. The teeth were flat on the sides, but sharp and **serrated** like steak knives at the front and back. The serrated edges helped the teeth easily slice through flesh.

Allosaurus also had three clawed fingers on each hand. His claws were more than 15 centimetres (6 inches) long. They were curved to a point like an eagle's talons. The claws helped Allosaurus grab on to even the largest dinosaurs. Allosaurus' natural weapons would be an advantage against any opponent.

prey animal that is hunted by another animal
serrated having a jagged edge

BRACHIOSAURUS' WEAPONS

Brachiosaurus
Huge feet, neck, and tail
★ ★

Brachiosaurus was a **herbivore**. He had few weapons to defend himself. His main weapon was his enormous size. He was big enough to stamp on an attacker. Catching an enemy's leg or tail under his huge foot could cause it serious harm.

herbivore animal that eats only plants

Brachiosaurus had five toes on each foot. One toe on each front foot had a hooked claw. Three toes on each back foot also had claws. These claws weren't as long or as nasty as Allosaurus' claws, but they were long and sharp enough to be dangerous in a fight.

Brachiosaurus also had a long, heavy tail and neck. Getting hit with either one could knock even a big predator like Allosaurus off his feet.

Brachiosaurus' thigh bone was more than 1.8 metres (6 feet) long.

FIERCE FACT BONES

ATTACK STYLE

Allosaurus
Swift and violent

★ ★ ★ ★ ★

★ ★ ★

Brachiosaurus
Slow but powerful

When attacking, Allosaurus struck quickly and often. His strong, "S"-shaped neck allowed him to dart his head forwards like a snake. His strong jaw helped him tear away strips of flesh from his prey. He would take shallow bites out of his victim until it grew weak from losing blood. Then he could finish his meal.

Brachiosaurus was a peaceful plant-eater. He didn't attack other dinosaurs. However, when under attack, he swung his neck and tail like giant clubs to keep predators away. He could also kick at the attacking predators or stamp on them with his huge, heavy feet. Brachiosaurus probably wasn't very quick, but when he hit an enemy it would cause serious damage.

GET READY TO RUMBLE!

When the earth shakes under your feet, you'll know this battle is on! It's a clash of the meanest and the mightiest, and there's bound to be some pain. In one corner is the frightening and aggressive predator – Allosaurus! He's the most vicious meat-eater of his time, and he likes a good fight. In the other corner is his brawny opponent – Brachiosaurus! He isn't looking for a fight, but he's big enough to take out his enemies. This fight is bound to be one for the ages!

ALLOSAURUS

SIZE ★★★☆
★★★★★

DEFENCES ★★★
★★★

WEAPONS ★★★★★
★★

ATTACK STYLE ★★★★★
★★★

BRACHIOSAURUS

You've got a front row seat. So sit back, turn the page, and get ready to enjoy the battle!

ONE LAST THING...

These two dinosaurs might have battled in real life. But this fight is made up. No one has ever seen these two mighty beasts go head-to-head. There's no way to know how it would have happened. Still, if you like a good dinosaur showdown, this one should be really amazing!

THE BATTLE

Deep, round footprints criss-cross a lakeside clearing. The leafy treetops nearby are cropped short, chewed by a herd of hungry dinosaurs. Several tall heads poke above the trees.

In the clearing, a lone Brachiosaurus lowers his long neck to sip some cool water. Suddenly, he stops. He hears footsteps. He jerks his head up and cranes his neck to peer into the woods.

Suddenly, a knife-toothed Allosaurus steps out of the woods. He stands about as tall as Brachiosaurus' legs. He stares hungrily at the meaty herbivore.

FIERCE FACT

PACK HUNTERS

Some fossil sites of plant-eating dinosaurs also contain fossils from several different Allosauruses. Some scientists believe these sites prove that Allosaurus hunted in packs.

Then a second, larger Allosaurus steps out of the woods. The first Allosaurus snarls at the newcomer. The larger predator roars and curls his clawed fingers. The first Allosaurus growls and turns his attention back to Brachiosaurus.

Suddenly, all three dinosaurs charge! The two predators run towards Brachiosaurus, who barrels straight ahead. The three beasts clash at the centre of the clearing. The impact sends the two meat-eaters flying like bowling pins.

Brachiosaurus keeps running until he reaches the edge of the clearing. The woods are too thick for his giant body. He stops and turns around. His enemies have climbed to their feet and are facing him once more. The Allosauruses open their deadly mouths wide and roar. This battle is about to get nasty!

Brachiosaurus ate the leaves of gingko trees. Many smaller herbivores ate ferns as well as other plants.

FIERCE FACT FOOD

Brachiosaurus runs. The two attackers chase after him. The ground shakes as Brachiosaurus' feet pound the earth.

The two meat-eaters come up behind him, one at each hip. They snap at his body, slicing their knife-like teeth into his flesh. Using their strong necks, they tear chunks of flesh from his side. Blood oozes from the wounds.

Brachiosaurus wails. He stops and whips his tail at his attackers. He lands a blow on the smaller Allosaurus. It tumbles backwards and skids across the ground. The larger Allosaurus strikes again and catches Brachiosaurus on the tail. Again, Brachiosaurus wails.

Brachiosaurus starts to run. But the larger Allosaurus heads him off. He snaps at the herbivore's meaty front leg. Brachiosaurus kicks at his enemy with his clawed foot. The Allosaurus screeches and backs away. A deep gash runs down his back leg.

Brachiosaurus turns away from the predator and rumbles back towards the lake. He finds the smaller Allosaurus standing in front of him. The smaller foe charges, but Brachiosaurus is ready. He swings his long, thick neck and wallops the attacker, who tumbles to the ground again.

Brachiosaurus thunders across the clearing. The larger Allosaurus races after his prey. Brachiosaurus whips his long tail at the approaching predator, but the Allosaurus ducks under the blow. Then he digs his long, sharp claws into Brachiosaurus' flesh.

While gripping the massive prey, the large Allosaurus snaps down on his victim's back. He rips out another big chunk of flesh. Brachiosaurus howls in pain.

The name Allosaurus means "different lizard".

FIERCE FACT

NAME

Brachiosaurus begins to feel weak. He starts to panic. He thrashes his head and tail at the creature latched onto his back. He wails, bucks, and shakes.

Brachiosaurus steps into the lake with his back foot. He tries to pull himself forwards, but the large Allosaurus, still clamped on, bites again. Brachiosaurus jerks backwards and loses his balance. He topples sideways and plunges into the lake. He lands on top of his enemy. The larger Allosaurus is crushed beneath his prey's massive weight.

The lake water reaches halfway up Brachiosaurus' body. He is stuck in the thick mud at the bottom of the lake. Weakened by the attack, Brachiosaurus can't climb out. The water turns red where he lies.

At the edge of the lake, the smaller Allosaurus hungrily eyes the fallen Brachiosaurus. He lets out a triumphant screech. He'll have a feast today!

GLOSSARY

evolve when something develops over a long time with gradual changes

extinct no longer living; an extinct animal is one whose kind has died out completely.

fossil remains or traces of plants and animals that are preserved as rock

herbivore animal that eats only plants

herd group of the same kind of animal

predator animal that hunts other animals for food

prey animal hunted by another animal for food

serrated having a jagged edge that helps with cutting, such as a saw

FIND OUT MORE

BOOKS

Dinosaur Encyclopedia, Caroline Bingham
(Dorling Kindersley, 2007)

Dinosaur Hunters: Palaeontologists, Louise and
Richard Spilsbury (Heinemann Library, 2007)

Prehistoric Scary Creatures, John Malam
(Book House, 2008)

WEBSITE

www.nhm.ac.uk/kids-only/dinosaurs
Visit the Natural History Museum's website to discover
more than 300 types of dinosaur, play dinosaur games,
and find out what sort of dinosaur you would be!

PLACES TO VISIT

Dinosaur Isle
Sandown, Isle of Wight PO36 8QA
www.dinosaurisle.com

Natural History Museum
London SW7 5BD
www.nhm.ac.uk

The Dinosaur Museum
Dorchester DT1 1EW
www.thedinosaurmuseum.com

INDEX